INDIA
UNDER INDIRA
AND RAJIV
GANDHI

INDIA
UNDER INDIRA
AND RAJIV
GANDHI

James Haskins

E N SLOW PUBLISHERS, INC.

Bloy St. & Ramsey Ave.	P.O. Box 38
Box 777	Aldershot
Hillside, N. J. 07205	Hants GU12 6BP
U.S.A.	U.K.

Library of Congress Cataloging-in-Publication Data

Haskins, James 1941-
   India under Indira and Rajiv Gandhi / by James Haskins.
     p. cm.
   Bibliography: p.
   Includes index.
   Summary: Chronicles the recent history of India under Indira
Gandhi and her son Rajiv as they have pursued the goal of a strong,
united India.
   ISBN 0-89490-146-X
   1. India—History—1947- —Juvenile literature. 2. Gandhi,
Indira, 1917-1984—Juvenile literature. 3. Gandhi, Rajiv, 1944- -
-Juvenile literature. [1. India—History—1947- 2. Gandhi,
Indira, 1917-1984. 3. Gandhi, Rajiv, 1944- .] I. Title.
DS480.84.H34414 1989
954.05'092'2—dc19   88-21209
                                                           CIP
                                                            AC
Printed in the United States of America

10 9 8 7 6 5 4 3 2 1

ILLUSTRATION CREDITS:
AP/Wide World Photos: pp. 20, 27, 35, 40, 47, 60, 63, 71, 73, 77, 79 (top and bot-
tom), 87, 93; Compliments of the Consul General of India, p. 51 and cover.

To Artisha

ACKNOWLEDGMENTS

I am grateful to Ann Kalkhoff and Kathy Benson for their help.

Contents

"It may be said of the Indian situation that if you are not confused, you are not well-informed."

Nani A. Palkhivala

1

Mother to Son

On October 31, 1984, Prime Minister Indira Gandhi of India was assassinated in her own garden by one of her own bodyguards. Her son, Rajiv, stepped in to take her place. He was forty years old and new to Indian politics. He had run for office for the first time only three years before and was in his third year in the Indian Parliament. Until the age of thirty-six, he had never shown the slightest interest in politics. His younger brother, Sanjay, was the politician and the person their mother had hoped would one day succeed her. But Sanjay had died in a plane crash in 1980, leaving Rajiv as the only son.

In December 1984 Rajiv Gandhi was formally inaugurated as the new prime minister of India. Barely over mourning the death of his mother, he faced the huge job of governing a country that was torn by religious and class hatred. His mother had died because of that hatred, and Rajiv knew that he, too, was in danger. In addition, India was a huge country of seven hundred fifty million people with great gaps between rich and poor and with too many people to feed. It was a

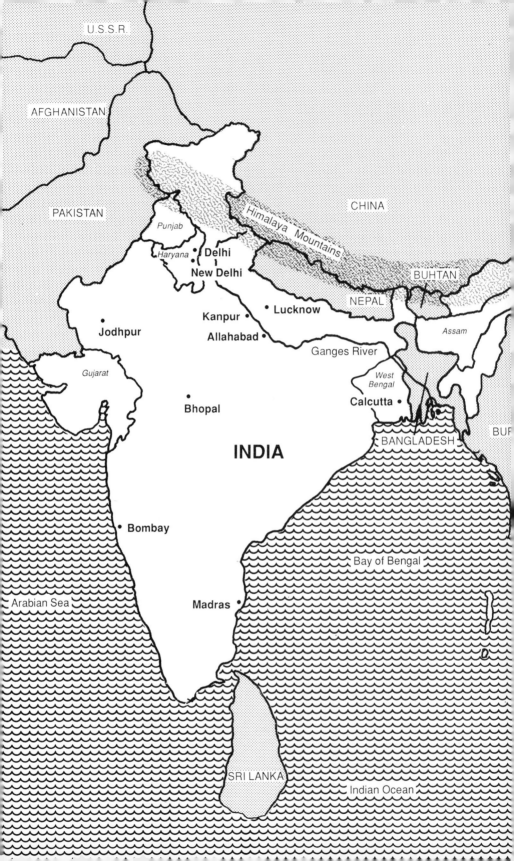

country with a government that did not work. Trying to lead such a country would be a huge task.

Rajiv Gandhi had spent most of his life wanting to be a pilot for Indian Airlines. He had entered politics because of the death of his brother and because he felt that, as he said at the time, "Mummy has to be helped somehow." Family loyalty is strong in Rajiv Gandhi. In politics, the family line is as old as the nation of India. Rajiv's grandfather, Jawaharlal Nehru, was India's first prime minister. After his death, his daughter and Rajiv's mother, Indira Gandhi, became prime minister. Now, Rajiv Gandhi was prime minister. No wonder people talked about a family political dynasty.

But Rajiv Gandhi did not want to be simply part of a family dynasty. Now that he was prime minister, he wanted to make his mark on history as an individual, too. That was going to be a big job.

2

Midnight's Child

Rajiv Gandhi was born on August 20, 1944. His father, Feroze Gandhi, was a newspaperman. His mother, Indira Gandhi, was the only child of one of the most important men in India. At the time Rajiv was born, Jawaharlal Nehru was in prison.

Nehru had devoted his life to gaining the independence of India from Great Britain, which had ruled the country for 200 years. He had been a follower of Mohandas K. Gandhi, the man who had led millions of Indians in nonviolent protest against British rule. Nehru had joined Gandhi in these protests, and he had been arrested and jailed many times during the more than twenty-five years of civil disobedience against the British in India. Gandhi, whose followers called him the Mahatma, or Great Soul, led a political party called the Indian National Congress party. Nehru joined that party and became one of its leaders.

Indira Gandhi and her husband also joined the party and the struggle against British rule. She and Feroze Gandhi (no relation to Mohandas K. Gandhi) had met and fallen in love when he was eighteen and she thirteen. Three years later, Feroze had proposed, but they had put off marriage. Feroze had to take care of his mother, and both he and Indira were so involved in the struggle for independence that it was not until the early spring of 1942, when Indira was twenty-five, that they finally got married. They moved into a small, half-finished house in Allahabad, thinking they would complete it gradually. However, they were both so busy organizing protests against the British that they barely saw each other. Often, they would not get home until midnight or later. They even put off their honeymoon until they had more time.

When they finally did take a honeymoon trip to the province of Kashmir a few months after their marriage, they cut their trip short to return to the city of Bombay, where Jawaharlal Nehru was leading another protest. It was the fall of 1942. Nehru was arrested and jailed. Indira and Feroze were also arrested and imprisoned without trial. Indira was released after nine months because of ill health, but Feroze stayed in prison for a year. After his release, they resumed their political activities as well as their married life. The following year, 1944, their first son was born.

Indira Gandhi wrote later that when Rajiv was born, "I think it was one of the most joyful moments in my life, although I must say at the time he seemed quite ugly." Nevertheless, she took him as soon as she could to the British prison where her father was confined and proudly held the infant up to the cell bars so Jawaharlal Nehru could see his first grandchild. Being in prison did not stop the older man from playing his role as head of the family. He consulted everyone in the jail about what his daughter and son-in-law should call their first child.

Nehru named the infant Rajivaratna. It was a combination of "lotus" for the name of the child's grandmother, Kamala

16

(Nehru's late wife, who had died in 1936), and "gem," for the first three syllables of his grandfather's name, Jawaharlal. It was a hopeful name for a little boy born in a time of turmoil. World War II was in progress, and Great Britain was busy defending itself against Germany. Indians saw a chance to push their fight for independence from Britain.

Rajiv Gandhi was a happy baby. His mother and father doted on him. His mother was especially determined that her child would have all the love and affection that she felt she had not had from parents who were so busy in the independence struggle that they had not paid much attention to their daughter. Both Indira and Feroze Gandhi played with Rajiv and cuddled him, and Rajiv laughed and smiled. And when his parents learned that India would finally be free, they must have shared their joy with him, although he was far too young to understand the reason for their celebration.

After World War II ended, Great Britain was ready to give up control of India, but the British wanted to leave behind a region that was stable and friendly. They didn't see how they could do that when India itself was so deeply divided along religious lines.

The majority of people on the Indian subcontinent were Hindus, followers of an ancient faith that had developed over a period of about four thousand years. But there was a good-sized minority of Moslems. During the 700s, Arab Moslems conquered the northwestern Indian province of Sind. They made further headway beginning around 1000 A.D., and again in the 1500s. From the 1600s to the 1830s, the Hindus were in power again. All this time, the Moslems and Hindus lived side by side quite peacefully.

Then the British came, and they gained control of most of the Indian subcontinent. Under the British, great hatred between Hindus and Moslems began to arise. The more edu-

17

cated and affluent Indians were mostly Hindus. They adopted English ways and learned the English language. In return, the British favored them and gave them more influence in the government. Before long, the Hindus were the privileged class.

The most privileged among them were the maharajahs, or rajs. Before British rule, these Indian princes had enjoyed great power and were fierce warriors, always fighting for territory among themselves. They had the power of life and death over their subjects. The British took away these powers, but allowed the maharajahs and their families to live in great wealth and comfort.

The Moslems held fast to their traditions. They were less likely to learn English or English ways. They were the second-class citizens of India and had little voice in running the country.

Both Hindus and Moslems wanted India to be independent from Britain. But each group was worried about the other in an independent India. Mohandas Gandhi, who was a Hindu, tried to get Moslems involved in his nonviolent protest against British rule, but most of his followers were Hindus. Jawaharlal Nehru was a Hindu. The Hindus wanted an independent state of India in which Hindus held the power. The Moslems wanted their own state.

Back in 1930 a Moslem Indian, named Sir Mohammed Iqbal, had proposed that India be separated into two states, one Hindu and one Moslem. After World War II, Moslems tried to persuade the British that such a division of India would be the best way to guarantee the safety and stability of the Indian subcontinent.

The British were not sure that such a division was the best thing, and they tried to come up with a better way. In the meantime, they released most of the Indian political prisoners and started the country on the road to independence. Jawaharlal Nehru was named to head the new interim government of India.

Before he even went to the capital, New Delhi, which the British had built near the city of Delhi in 1912, Nehru appointed his son-in-law, Feroze Gandhi, managing editor of the newspaper *The National Herald,* in Lucknow. Feroze, Indira, and Rajiv moved to Lucknow. Indira was pregnant again, but she felt that her father needed help in Delhi, and soon she took little Rajiv and went there to be with him. It was in Delhi that her second son was born in December 1946. Jawaharlal Nehru named the little boy Sanjay, which means "victory."

After the birth of Sanjay, Indira returned with her sons to Lucknow. For little Rajiv Gandhi, there was too much change all at once. The moves back and forth were hard enough, but now there was a new baby. Rajiv was no longer the center of attention. He resented Sanjay and demanded from his mother more attention than she could give. She later wrote that he had tantrums, but that scolding him only made matters worse.

With two sons now, Indira Gandhi tried to continue being a mother who was always there. She did not want her children brought up by nannies and nurses, as she had been. But by this time, her thoughts were often in Delhi with her father. She wondered how he was getting along without someone to care for him. He had sisters living with him in the prime minister's residence, but Indira Gandhi thought he needed more help than they could give.

The Indian Independence Act was signed in 1947, and Britain officially gave up all claims to the Indian subcontinent. But at the same time, to please the Moslem minority in India, the British also created a separate Moslem state—Pakistan, Land of the Pure. Since it was created for religious reasons, not geographical ones, this new state had very odd borders. It consisted of two regions—East Bengal (later East Pakistan) and West Pakistan. These two parts of the new state were separated by more than a thousand miles.

Few people, inside or outside India, believed that this kind of division would work. But for the time being, it seemed the only solution. At midnight on August 15, 1947, the Indian subcontinent became officially free of British rule, and the independent states of India and Pakistan were born.

An Indian writer named Salman Rushdie later wrote a novel about India called *Midnight's Children.* It was about the

Four-year-old Rajiv Gandhi appears with his grandfather, Prime Minister Jawaharlal Nehru, on the grounds of the Prime Minister's House.

generation of Indians born on or shortly after that night of August 15, 1947—a generation born into an independent India. It was about the odd circumstances of a people who could trace their roots back five thousand years in a country that had never before existed as an independent state. Many people call Rajiv Gandhi one of those "midnight children." He was five days short of his third birthday when the new white, gold, and green national flag of India was hoisted, so he was not one of those born at midnight on August 15, 1947, or shortly thereafter. But a three-year-old child was too young to remember the struggle for India's independence. He was part of the new generation of people who would know only an independent India.

After official independence, Indira Gandhi began commuting between Lucknow and Delhi, a night's journey by train and one not at all to Rajiv's liking. He already resented the attention she gave to Sanjay; now she was going off to Delhi all the time. His father was attentive and was always making wooden toys for him, but his father was not a replacement for his mother.

His mother, meanwhile, was having a hard time maintaining such a demanding schedule, and her older son's tantrums did not help. She later wrote that she decided to try reasoning with him. She told him that she loved him but that his crying disturbed her. Little Rajiv told her that he couldn't help crying, that the crying just came. She said to him, "There is a nice fountain in the garden. When you want to cry or shout, go to the fountain and do it there." From then on, at the first sign of tears from Rajiv, his mother would whisper "fountain," and he would go away. She believed that at the fountain he became interested in a flower or the falling water and forgot his troubles.

After a while, Indira Gandhi realized that the commute

was too tiring. She decided to leave Lucknow and take the boys to Delhi to live in the prime minister's residence. Her husband did not try to stop her. He realized that being with her father was something she must do.

The prime minister's official residence was called Teen Murti House (House of Three Statues). Before independence, it had been the house of the British commander-in-chief. It had large, cold rooms full of huge oil paintings of famous British generals and heroes. Indira Gandhi had these paintings moved to a warehouse, and she redecorated the mansion in Indian style. Although it was still a very large and formal place, it became more lively after Indira began inviting politicians, artists, and old friends to visit. She acted as her father's official hostess and could not spend as much time with her children as before. She put them in the charge of Anna Orsholt, a Danish governess who had worked for the Nehru family for several years.

Both Rajiv and Sanjay were already used to meeting important people and being waited on by servants, and this move made no great difference in their lives. They missed their father, though, and Indira Gandhi made it a point to take them back to Lucknow for regular visits. After a time, Feroze Gandhi realized that journeying back and forth was a hardship for her, and he began visiting Delhi more often. But he never felt comfortable in the home of Jawaharlal Nehru. His father-in-law clearly had more influence over his family than he did, and Feroze felt like a stranger. As time went on, he visited less often.

Rajiv and Sanjay were privileged children. When their mother felt she, and they, needed a change, she would take them to the president's cottage, which was really a huge house with ten or eleven bedrooms, in a place called Mashobra via Simla. When they were young, the boys thought all children had the kind of life they did. They did not know about the great poverty in which the majority of their countrymen lived. Nor did they know what turmoil their country was in.

The whole transfer of power from the British to the two new states of India and Pakistan was badly organized. Almost immediately, the two governments started fighting over boundaries. Both claimed the northern province of Kashmir. While the majority of people there were Moslems, the government was Hindu. Indian and Pakistani troops fought for years in the small mountainous region, but neither side was able to win a clear victory.

Meanwhile, in the areas that were not disputed, the two new governments were setting up their capitals. India had fewer problems—its new leaders took over the government that the British had already put in place. But Pakistan began with practically nothing. Government records had to be moved from India's capital of Delhi to Pakistan's makeshift capital at Karachi. Such a move was the least of the problems facing the new government, however.

Millions of Moslems and Hindus had to leave their homes. Most Moslems, who lived in the territory that was now India, moved to the territory that was now Pakistan. The same was true for Hindus who happened to live in the two regions that were now Pakistan. More than seven million Moslems moved from India to Pakistan, and ten million Hindus went to India from Pakistan. The panic and rioting that resulted took more than a million lives.

Rajiv got a glimpse of the rioting only once in his early years. In 1947 his mother had taken him and Sanjay to a mountain resort, and on the way back to Delhi, their train stopped in a suburb of the capital called Shahdara. They looked out the window and saw a mob preparing to hang a Moslem right on the train platform. Leaving her frightened sons on the train, Indira Gandhi charged out onto the platform and managed to talk the mob into leaving peacefully, thus saving the life of one Moslem.

Another man lost his life during that time of riot and unrest—Mohandas K. Gandhi, the little man who had done so much to bring about independence from Britain through nonviolent protest. He was assassinated on January 30, 1948, less than six months after independence, by Hindu extremists who were against partition of the Indian subcontinent.

Rajiv Gandhi saw the Mahatma the day before the assassination. His mother took him with her on a visit, along with her aunt and a cousin. As the adults talked, little Rajiv made flower chains and decorated the Mahatma's feet with them. The next day, he learned that the beloved old man was gone. Rajiv was not quite four and a half and did not understand what had happened or why.

3

A Privileged Childhood

It is not likely that young Rajiv Gandhi knew very much, if anything, about the conflict between India and Pakistan, but he was now old enough to sense when there was tension in the household. After the assassination of Mohandas Gandhi, there was much tension, for the new, independent Indian state was very fragile. Nehru worked hard to give all Indians a stake in the new democratic state. He abolished all royal titles and vowed that the new constitution would not make distinctions because of birth or social standing. He put great store in the power of a new constitution, and his daughter acted as hostess at many meetings to discuss its provisions. It was finally completed in November 1949.

The new constitution was democratic and was modeled after the British system of government. It called for a federal union of states that was firmly held together by a strong national government. The center of this government was the prime minister and a council of ministers, who were chosen from among the members of a central parliament. The constitution called for a supreme court and a president as guardians of good government. Neither the supreme court nor the president was to have the power of checks and balances they have in a government that is set up like that of the United States.

The new constitution called for periodic general elections, and the first free elections in independent India were held in 1952. Jawaharlal Nehru's Congress party, which was much stronger than a mere political party, had proved its patriotism in the struggle against British rule and won the majority of the seats in Parliament. Its plurality helped to stabilize the new country.

By that time, Indira Gandhi had enrolled both her sons in school. The Shiv Niketan (Abode of Serentity) was a local elementary school where the students were taught in the Hindi language and learned arts and crafts and general knowledge. Their classmates were the children of other well-to-do Indians in politics and business. One reason why the boys were enrolled there was that the school did not emphasize the Hindu religion. Their grandfather believed that India had to go beyond the strict religion of Hinduism, that the new generation must learn to have a wider vision.

In their grandfather's house, the boys could not help acquiring that wider vision. In fact, they must have grown up believing that politics, not religion, was the basis for many actions. They lived around power. Representatives from governments around the world came to call on Jawaharlal Nehru. Both the East (Russia and other Communist countries) and the West (the United States and the other democratic countries of Europe) wanted the huge new nation to be an ally. While Nehru's official policy was one of nonalignment, in those early days he depended heavily on the United States for aid.

As the grandchildren of Jawaharlal Nehru, Rajiv and Sanjay were also "the nation's grandchildren." They were used to appearing in official photographs, attending ceremonies, and receiving gifts.

They even had their own private zoo! Actually, it was their grandfather's. Nehru loved animals, and many people gave gifts of animals to the prime minister. In addition to dogs, parrots and other birds, rabbits, and squirrels, there was a red Himalayan panda cub that Rajiv took to immediately. He named it Bhimsa, and for quite some time it lived in Rajiv's bathroom. But it refused to be house trained and was always racing around the house. Eventually, his mother banished Bhimsa to the garden.

Rajiv and Sanjay accompanied their mother and grandfather on an official trip to Germany in 1956.

Later on, the people of Assam gave the prime minister a mate for Bhimsa. She was named Poma. Pandas usually do not mate in captivity, but Bhimsa and Poma did, producing cubs that the boys and their grandfather adored.

When Rajiv was about eleven, three tiger cubs came to live in the Nehru zoo. He and Sanjay played with them as if they were house cats and laughed when other people showed fear. Unfortunately, the cubs grew quickly, and soon two of them had to go to the Lucknow Zoo. Nehru gave the third to Marshal Tito of Yugoslavia, who had admired it.

While the boys were certainly having much wider experiences than most Indian children, in some ways their vision of the world was narrower. They were so privileged, so accustomed to power, that they did not know what it was like to go without. By this time, even their father was a politician. Feroze Gandhi had campaigned for and won election to a parliamentary seat from Rae Bareli, near Lucknow in Uttar Pradesh. He declined to move into the prime minister's residence with his wife and sons, but he did move to Delhi and lived in a small house provided to members of parliament.

Although their father was now nearer and made a point of visiting the boys as often as he could, he was busy with parliamentary business. Their mother was of course deeply involved in politics and her father's administration. Therefore, by the time Rajiv was twelve, his parents and grandfather had decided that he and Sanjay should go to boarding school. After all, most upper-class Indian boys did. Their elders wanted Rajiv and Sanjay to get a well-rounded education with other boys of similar economic and social backgrounds.

Both Rajiv and Sanjay were sent to the Doon School, in the foothills of the Himalayas. Founded in 1927 when the British still ruled India, it educated the sons of Hindu civil servants and merchants who one day would lead an independent India. The Doon School wanted to produce "all-around boys" who were well educated, as well as sports- and outdoor-minded. The headmaster at the time, J. A. K. Martyn, was a great mountain climber, and he made sure that all the boys went on long and strenuous climbs. Also, the philosophy of the school was that the boys should realize that there were people in the world less fortunate than they. Doon School boys even worked with "untouchables" in the nearby village.

In the complicated caste system of traditional Hindu society, the untouchables were the lowest. There were four main classes or groups—priests, warriors, merchants and craftsmen, and servants. Within each class were various castes, each of which had its own standards of conduct, traditions, and way of life. The untouchables were so low that they weren't even in the system. They were the cleaners and scavengers. They had to live and eat apart from other castes. If a priest as much as saw an untouchable on a street, he would return home at once to wash this "pollution" away. In some regions of India, untouchables had to wear bells to warn others that they were coming. Untouchables could only marry other untouchables. They had few rights, only duties. They could not go to school, they could not own property, and the only jobs they could have were in sanitation, tanning, and shoemaking. The last two trades involved working in leather, and in Hindu India, where the cow is sacred, such jobs were considered distasteful. Needless to say, the untouchables were the most pitiful people in India, the poorest in a poor land.

Mahatma Gandhi had tried to persuade Indian society to end the cruel caste system that had produced a class like the untouchables. "The moment untouchability goes, the caste system itself will be purified," he said. He started calling them "Harijans" or "Children of God." He invited hundreds of them to go with him as he traveled around India. He ate with them and took them to political rallies and protest marches. But it was very hard to change the old traditions. It took Gandhi ten years to ensure that Harijans could worship inside Hindu temples.

By the time Rajiv Gandhi enrolled at the Doon School, his grandfather was trying to remove these strong barriers of class and caste and to make a better life for all Indians. The new Indian constitution, drafted in 1949, formally outlawed untouchability. The national government decreed that special jobs be set aside for untouchables in public businesses and government-owned industries like Air India. But the traditions were long and strong, and it has been difficult to change the caste system.

Both Rajiv and Sanjay liked the Doon School. Sanjay was the more outgoing, and he made friends there who would remain his buddies for the rest of his life. Rajiv was quieter, but he, too, enjoyed being there.

At the Doon School, the boys were taught in English, but they also learned about Indian culture. They learned hymns in Sanskrit, the traditional Indian written language. Though they learned to appreciate their Indian heritage, they were taught that the caste system was wrong. And they were also taught that politics was not a career for gentlemen, the reason being that many politicians in India had used India's caste and religious divisions for their own benefit and not for the good of the country. Rajiv's grandfather was different, of course. Although the boys were never treated in a special way, no teacher at the Doon School would dare suggest that Prime Minister Nehru was a mere politician. Still, Rajiv Gandhi grew up not liking politics very much.

He wanted to be a pilot. From his earliest years, he and his father had enjoyed playing with mechanical toys, especially airplanes. At the Doon School, he liked math and science and continued to dream of being a pilot. His parents and his grandfather encouraged him. No shadow of a career in politics loomed in his life.

In fact, very few shadows fell upon Rajiv Gandhi until 1960, when he was sixteen and his father died of a heart attack. Over the years, Feroze Gandhi and his wife had drifted apart. Although for some time he had not lived with his family, he had remained in close touch, and his sons were extremely upset by his death. Perhaps because of all those childhood trips to the fountain, Rajiv suffered quietly and did not show his emotions easily. Sanjay was more open in his grief. Their mother grieved as well. Though she and her husband had not gotten along very well, they had never stopped loving each other. The death of Feroze Gandhi left a big void in all their lives.

4

College Years

By the time his father died, Rajiv Gandhi was approaching the end of his career at the Doon School. His mother now worried about his higher education. He was not interested in an academic career, but his grandfather wanted at least one of his grandsons to follow in his footsteps and attend Cambridge University in England. As the older son and as a better student than Sanjay, Rajiv was the logical choice.

At the time, the Indian government was discouraging Indian students from going abroad. The main reason was economics. Students who went abroad had to pay their expenses in foreign currency, and the government needed that foreign currency to pay its own bills. Students wishing to study in Britain or the United States had a hard time doing so, and some in the Indian government believed that these same restrictions should apply to the "nation's grandchildren." But Indira Gandhi wanted her children to get the education that she had not had, and she was determined that they would study in England.

Rajiv enrolled at Cambridge's Trinity College, where his

grandfather had gone. It was his first long stint away from his homeland, but he was used to being on his own and accustomed to the English language and to British ways.

At Cambridge, he was not as well known as he had been at the Doon School, and he seemed to like things that way. Occasionally, someone would ask if he was related to Mohandas Gandhi, and he would answer that he was not. But he would not offer the information that he was the grandson of Prime Minister Nehru. Years later, he recalled, "My grandfather visited school while I was there, and I just disappeared. They couldn't find me. I was staying away from publicity and the limelight."

Quiet and modest, he was well liked at the school, though he was not a particularly good student. His mother was not so concerned about his grades as she was about the kind of man he was becoming. In the fall of 1962, she visited him for two days. She wrote to her friend in America, Dorothy Norman, "It is rather a poignant moment, isn't it, for a mother when her child becomes a man and she knows that he is no longer dependent on her and that from now on he will lead his own life which she may or may not be allowed to glimpse. . . . As for Rajiv, I can only hope and pray that he will have the strength to face and accept life in all its varied facets."

Two years later, Rajiv had to call on his inner strength to accept the death of his grandfather. Jawaharlal Nehru was seventy-four years old when he died in 1964. He had been in ill health since 1962. In January 1964 he suffered a serious stroke. In May, he suffered another and died soon afterward. Thus, his death was not unexpected. But for almost every Indian alive, his death was a national tragedy, for he was the symbol of the independent nation and of the struggle that had achieved that independence. There was national mourning, and there was family mourning. Indira Gandhi and Sanjay

Often Rajiv and Sanjay greeted their mother on her return from a trip abroad.

were quite emotional over the death. Rajiv was extremely upset, but friends recall that he did not talk about the loss with many people. He was simply quieter than usual for a few days.

Nehru had left strict instructions that he was not to be given a religious funeral, but his daughter did not honor those instructions. Her critics said that she wanted to capitalize on the sympathy she would get as the grieving daughter. Her supporters said she believed that the people needed to say good-bye to Jawaharlal Nehru with some kind of ceremony. She gave him a traditional Hindu funeral, and leaders from around the world attended.

As soon as the news of his death was announced, the Indian government took steps to name his successor. Nehru had not wanted to encourage any kind of family dynasty. He had once written to his younger sister that he felt such a dynasty would be "wholly undemocratic and undesirable." After his death, there was no real talk about his daughter succeeding him. She had the experience, but she did not have the power to bring about her own election. Nehru was succeeded by Shri Lal Bahadur Shastri, who was one of the senior leaders of the Congress party.

Prime Minister Shastri appointed Indira Gandhi Minister of Information and Broadcasting (by now TV was becoming important in India and to the government of India, so that television and radio were officially part of the responsibilities of that office). According to A. M. Rosenthal of *The New York Times,* who was that newspaper's correspondent in India from 1954 to 1958, "It was not much of a job, and to this day Indian politicians say she got the job not because she was powerful, but because she was powerless—Nehru had left her little estate, and she needed the job and the house in New Delhi that goes with ministerial posts. She seemed bent and always full of sorrow, not a figure of power at all."

One of Indira Gandhi's first projects as Minister of Information and Broadcasting was to mount a special traveling exhibition about her father, which was shown in New York and elsewhere. She traveled widely and sometimes took one of her sons with her for a special occasion. In April 1965, she took Rajiv with her to the coronation of the Chogyal of Sikkim, an Indian protectorate.

Rajiv was now twenty years old and had fallen in love. At Cambridge he had met Sonia Maino, the daughter of an Italian businessman. His mother was not happy about this attachment, for she wanted Rajiv to fall in love with an Indian girl. She asked him not to rush into anything, and apparently he honored her wishes. He and Sonia saw each other as often as they could, but they put off plans for marriage.

Rajiv left Cambridge without graduating and enrolled at the Imperial College of Science and Technology in London. There, in 1965, he obtained a degree in mechanical engineering. After graduation, he returned to India.

Sanjay, meanwhile, had not graduated from the Doon School. He had not been expelled, but the school authorities had suggested to his mother that he would be better off somewhere else. He had returned to the prime minister's residence in New Delhi and attended St. Columbus School there. While his brother loved airplanes, Sanjay loved cars. He declined to go to college but did consent to go to England to work as an apprentice at a Rolls-Royce dealership in the city of Crewe. Neither Rajiv nor Sanjay had any interest in politics, and at the time their mother did not encourage them to have such an interest.

As part of her job, Indira Gandhi enjoyed traveling and meeting new people, especially film and television stars. But she also did serious work. Family planning was very important to her, for she believed that the terrible poverty in India was due in part to the high birth rate. In the fall of 1965, she was busy raising funds to get low-cost radio receivers in rural areas so that the people there could listen to programs on family planning. Also, with the help of West Germany, her ministry was bringing television to schools and hospitals in New Delhi and was broadcasting educational programs, children's programs, and family planning programs. She had even bigger plans for educating the Indian population through radio and television, but her budget was not large enough to pay for them. She probably shared these plans with her sons, who had known radio and television for as long as they had been available in India and who understood as well as she did how powerful these media were.

Then, suddenly on January 10, 1966, Shri Lal Bahadur Shastri had a stroke in Tashkent and died. The prime minister's death was so unexpected that he had left no designated successor, and his Congress party did not know whom to elect to take his place. The aging leaders of that party wanted to stall for time by making someone a kind of stopgap prime minister until they could figure out who should be elected to that office for the long term. This stopgap prime minister had to be someone who could be easily influenced by them, but also someone who was widely known. They chose Indira Gandhi because she was the daughter of Jawaharlal Nehru and because they thought she would do whatever they wanted. They were wrong about the last part. The shy woman, who had always seemed to walk a few steps behind, not beside, her father, had a lot more substance than the Congress party leaders gave her credit for.

First, she took office. Then, she took power. It was a while before she realized that she had power simply because she was Nehru's daughter. Throughout India, there was great affection for her as the only child of the country's beloved father figure. That affection helped her to win the office of prime minister in her own right in the elections of February 1967. Indira traveled throughout India, as her father had done, and the crowds who gathered to get a glimpse of her made her realize that she had the backing of the majority of the Indian people.

But the people had only so much power in Indian politics. Even more powerful were the politicians, and the interests they represented. In that same election, the Congress party lost seats to two different Communist parties, one aligned with the Soviet Union and one aligned with Communist China. The two Socialist parties also gained seats in Parliament as a result of that election. The Congress party still held a majority of seats, but now it was vulnerable to combinations of opposition parties.

Sanjay had returned to India by this time, and when Indira became prime minister, both he and Rajiv moved with her to the prime minister's official residence, where both boys had spent many of their growing-up years. Rajiv was still not interested in politics. His chief interest was Sonia Maino. Eventually, Indira Gandhi realized that the two were deeply in love, and she consented to their marriage. The wedding took place in 1968, amid great pageantry, and Indira Gandhi welcomed her new daughter-in-law to the prime minister's residence. She came to love Sonia. She wrote to Dorothy Norman in the United States in May 1969, "Apart from being beautiful, Sonia is a really nice girl, wholesome and straightforward."

The following summer Rajiv and Sonia's first child, a son whom they named Rahul, was born. A little girl, Priyana, was born the following year. Rajiv was then attending pilot training school and hoping to work for Indian Airlines after he got his license. He became a commerical pilot in 1972 and got a job with the government-owned domestic airline. As a junior pilot, he flew twin-engine, propeller-driven planes between minor cities around India.

Sanjay was still pursuing his interest in automobiles. He may have considered working in the existing car industry in India, but he never actually took such a job. What he really wanted was his own car-manufacturing business. He had dreams of producing a small compact car for India that would be better than the Ambassador, the one Indian-made car available. The government wanted to encourage local industries, and there were such high tariffs (import taxes) on foreign cars that they basically were not available.

Sanjay already had the design of his dream car in mind, as well as the name. He wanted to call it Maruti, which means "Son of the Wind God" in Hindi. *And* he wanted to produce

Rajiv and Sonia, at center, attend a fashion show with Indira and Sanjay Gandhi.

it in partnership with the Indian government. He made official application to the government to build his car, but he was not the first to take such action. In the earlier cases the government had not come to a decision. The producers of the Ambassador had naturally been against the introduction of another car, especially a car produced in part with the backing of the government. Some in the government believed that India's precious resources for transportation should be spent on bicycles and new buses for public transportation, rather than on private automobiles.

But Sanjay's application was treated differently. In fact, he obtained government approval quickly. He then raised the money to buy land near Delhi for his factory. Anyone else would have taken years to accomplish what Sanjay did in a remarkably short time. No one ever accused Indira Gandhi of asking special favors for her younger son. But people did charge that she did not have to, that bureaucrats in the Indian government would be anxious to please her by helping her son. Her opponents tried to characterize the whole affair as a political scandal and a case of special favors for the prime minister's family, but they could not prevent construction from beginning on the Maruti plant.

Meanwhile, Indira Gandhi was working to consolidate her political power. Weakened in the 1967 elections, the Congress party began to split into factions. One faction was against Prime Minister Indira Gandhi and wanted her to step down. The other faction remained loyal to her and to her radical ideas about redistributing to the poor the land, most of which was owned by a rich few, and about nationalizing, or having the government take over, the banks. Mrs. Gandhi then took an even more radical step. She announced the formation of a new Congress party and scheduled elections for March 1971. She believed that she and her new party could win those elections, and they did, by a wide margin. After that, Indira Gandhi held undisputed power in India.

She also had a big responsibility to make good on her promises. The young and the poor now looked to her to take the actions that her power would allow.

One of her first acts was to sign a treaty of peace, friendship, and cooperation with the Soviet Union on August 9, 1971. She believed that India should not put all its eggs in one basket and rely only on the West for help in modernizing the country. Friendship with Communist Russia did not mean that she was turning her back on the United States. She continued to keep the lines of communication open to the West as well, although by later in the year those lines were under great strain.

The problem, again, was Pakistan, and the two separate geographical areas that were supposed to make up that country. East Pakistan had been plagued by unrest since partition and independence in 1947. Then called East Bengal, it was a thousand miles from West Pakistan, the center of government. Not until the 1950s was it renamed East Pakistan, and not until 1962 did a new constitution provide for a federal Islamic republic with two provinces (East and West Pakistan) and two official languages (Bengali and Urdu). Over the next ten years the people of East Pakistan were often discontented with the government of West Pakistan, and there was a rising sentiment for independence. On March 26, 1971, East Pakistan declared its independence as the country of Bangladesh. Troops from West Pakistan moved in immediately to put down the insurrection and occupy the region.

Mrs. Gandhi supported East Pakistan's independence, and in December 1971 she ordered troops into East Pakistan to fight West Pakistan troops. Thus, India and Pakistan were then at war. The war lasted less than two weeks and ended in the defeat of West Pakistan. The country of Bangladesh was thus established. Both the United States and China had supported West Pakistan in this brief war, and relations between those two countries and India were not good by the end of 1971.

Indira Gandhi had solidified her country's dominance over the Indian subcontinent. She had also proved that while she favored a democratic form of government, she was not above making friends with nondemocratic countries if she felt these friendships would benefit India.

5

Prime Minister's Son

Indira Gandhi believed that India should not have to rely on other countries for its own defense, and she ordered government scientists to undertake a program of nuclear research that would give India the ultimate weapon of warfare. In 1974, India entered the nuclear age when it exploded an underground nuclear device.

Three months after the end of the war that created Bangladesh, Mrs. Gandhi solidified her own power in India through elections that saw her Congress party capture more than 70 percent of the state assembly seats in regional elections.

Then events that were beyond her control took over. There were two severe droughts, and the world faced a serious oil crisis when the oil-producing states of the Middle East decided to show their power over the world economy by raising their prices drastically. Inflation in India soared. The government did not seem to have the ability to deal effectively with the economic crisis that resulted.

Indira Gandhi's response to the growing criticism of her

45

government was to become more authoritarian. Faced with strikes by workers and protests by students, she proclaimed emergency measures that allowed her security forces to arrest and imprison the dissidents. She even ordered the takeover of the small Indian protectorate of Sikkim in the Himalayas.

Meanwhile, Indira Gandhi had obviously begun to think about the future of the Nehru family line in Indian government. Her father might not have considered the idea of a family political dynasty, but she did. Her clear choice as her successor was her younger son, Sanjay.

There were several reasons why she favored Sanjay. For one, now that his mother was prime minister, Sanjay had become interested in politics. Rajiv was not and had made that clear. Rajiv was the quiet one, shy and soft-spoken. Sanjay was outgoing and brash.

Rajiv was content with his job as a pilot for Indian Airlines. By this time, he had graduated to flying more sophisticated Boeing jet planes and looked forward to the time when he would be a senior pilot. He and his wife enjoyed their children, led an active social life in New Delhi's diplomatic and business circles, and obviously had no interest in cultivating political friends.

Sanjay was more ambitious. He had secured a great amount of government and private money to build the factory to manufacture his Maruti. He promised that the car would not only be compact and easy to drive, but also inexpensive to run because it would not take a lot of gasoline. Unfortunately, the Maruti never materialized. As Tariq Ali, author of a book titled *An Indian Dynasty: The Story of the Nehru-Gandhi Family,* put it, "Sanjay was good at driving cars and fixing his own, but his performance as an industrialist had merely created a set of problems for his mother. . . . People began to ask what had been done with the money. No replies were forthcoming."

The differences between the two Gandhi sons extended even to their choices of wives. Rajiv had married a non-Indian. Any man who wanted to be powerful in India would have chosen an Indian wife.

Sanjay not only married an Indian; he married a Sikh, a member of a religious minority. From time to time, the Sikhs, who constituted the majority in the northern province of the Punjab, grew restless, and if Sanjay Gandhi had politics in mind when he chose a wife, he chose well. But he may simply have fallen in love with the young girl, Maneka Anand. Maneka's father was a retired army officer, who had been sta-

Once his mother became Prime Minister, Sanjay took an active roll in politics. Here he delivers a campaign speech.

tioned with his family in Great Britain for two years when Maneka was growing up. Her mother had studied psychology at the University of California at San Diego. Her parents were none too pleased when Maneka started dating Sanjay Gandhi, for she was only eighteen, and he was ten years older. She was still only eighteen when she married Sanjay Gandhi in a civil ceremony and moved into the prime minister's residence in Delhi. She continued her studies at the Jawaharlal Nehru University in Delhi and apparently was regarded by the rest of the family as young and opinionated. She later insisted that she had no interest in politics, only in being the bride of Sanjay Gandhi.

By the year following his marriage, Sanjay Gandhi was becoming more active in politics. Indira Gandhi was clearly moving her younger son into the limelight with her. He was pictured with her on posters and creating "photo opportunities" for himself. He had taken flying lessons and obtained his pilot's license. Now he was carrying on that family tradition as well, and the Indian press delighted in photographing him standing next to airplanes.

On the political front, Indira Gandhi was assigning him to perform duties in her name. And as that year wore on, she had more and more power and more and more duties to delegate.

Then, in June 1975, a court in Mrs. Gandhi's native Allahabad convincted her of electoral corruption—using government officials in her own election campaign—and said that her election as prime minister was invalid. The ruling questioned her right to remain in office and prohibited her from running in any election for six years. Her political opposition immediately called for her resignation.

Mrs. Gandhi refused to resign. Two days later she ordered the arrest and jailing of dozens of opposition leaders. She also proclaimed a state of emergency in India. She acted under a law that was a holdover from British rule, the Maintenance of National Security Act. This act gave her sweeping powers, and she used them. She ordered the arrest of thousands more people. She suspended India's version of the Bill of Rights. She censored the press. She suspended all the laws under which those who had been arrested could seek legal redress.

Her Congress party controlled Parliament, and when Parliament next convened, it changed the law under which she had been convicted in June. It also ratified the state of emergency.

Able now to push through whatever measures she wanted, Mrs. Gandhi announced strong new steps toward population control. To her mind, the only way to solve India's economic problems was to curb the growth of its population. At the end of 1975, Sanjay had been named to the executive committee of the Congress party's youth branch, and Mrs. Gandhi could now give him official duties. She assigned him to carry out her program, and he did more than perhaps even she had expected. One of his ideas was to encourage men to undergo voluntary sterilization. As a reward, these men received transistor radios.

Apparently, though, this tactic did not work. Soon Sanjay had ordered forced sterilization. According to Tariq Ali, "In August-September 1975 casual labourers had virtually disappeared from Delhi. This was unheard of in a city where there is always a rush to find work. The labourers, it was discovered, had returned to their villages to avoid [sterilization]. In November 1975 the Nehru birthday celebrations, which always included a large free picnic for hundreds of children, had to be cancelled. Mothers had refused to send their male children to the event in case 'Sanjay Gandhi's doctors' had them sterilised."

While few people agreed with Sanjay's tactics, in the year

49

1976 India had the best birth control record in its history.

Sanjay's critics charged that he encouraged his mother to forsake democracy and to create a dictatorship in India. They said that he was a "self-styled crown prince" and a "lawless power broker" who "hung around his doting mother like a dark and menacing shadow." According to Indian writer, Ved Mehta, author of a book called *A Family Affair,* "Rightly or wrongly, Sanjay was seen as representing the ruthless side of his mother."

Rajiv, meanwhile, did not step forward to represent his mother's more compassionate side. While he had little use for Sanjay's brand of politics, he did not feel there was anything he could do. He later told a friend that he had not heard much about the "excesses of the emergency," but what he had heard he had passed on to his family. They had refused to believe him. He did not press the issue, and went about his life as normally as he could. By now he was a senior pilot with Indian Airlines.

Indira Gandhi kept the conduct of foreign affairs for herself, although it is likely that she also consulted Sanjay in these matters as a way of educating him in international diplomacy. She established closer diplomatic ties with China. She also announced that India was officially a nonaligned country, although she seemed to favor the Soviet Union and to be cool toward the United States.

At the end of 1976, the government announced that because of the state of emergency new elections would not be held until early 1978. But in early 1977 Mrs. Gandhi changed her mind. In a surprise announcement, she scheduled elections in March because of her "unshakable faith" in the power of the people. Outside observers suggested that she was worried about her international reputation. She did not want to be known as a dictator. Also, she apparently believed

Indira Gandhi was a tough leader who inspired both great loyalty and great hatred.

that her Congress party would win the elections. Shortly after her announcement, she ordered the release of those political opponents who were still in jail.

The voters surprised her that March. They voted her out and elected her chief opponent, Morarji R. Desai, whom she had imprisoned at the end of 1975. Stunned, Indira Gandhi waited two days in the prime minister's residence before she finally emerged to hand in her resignation.

She and her family would now have to leave the prime minister's residence at 1 Safdarjung Road. This was a blow to Indira Gandhi, who had lived there for some thirty years. A Moslem friend named Mohammed Yunus came to the rescue. Back when India and Pakistan became two separate nations, he had been one of the few Moslems who had actually given up his home and moved to India because he wanted to be close to his friend Jawaharlal Nehru. He moved out of his house in Willingdon Crescent in New Delhi and gave it over to Indira Gandhi and her extended family.

Sonia Gandhi, for one, saw the need to move as an opportunity to leave her mother-in-law's household. Rajiv apparently agreed with her. He told his mother that he and Sonia and the children were going to leave India for a while and settle in Italy. Sonia had never applied for Indian citizenship and was still an Italian citizen; therefore, such a move would be fairly easy to accomplish. But Indira Gandhi could not take this new blow. She pleaded with both Rajiv and Sonia not to leave her at that time. She said she needed them, and her grandchildren, with her. Rajiv decided that he could not leave his mother, and Sonia went along with his wishes.

Later, friends of Sanjay charged that Rajiv and Sonia had wanted to leave because they did not believe Indira Gandhi could ever regain power. But there is no evidence that either Rajiv or Sonia had ever planned on gaining political power through Indira. Sonia, in fact, is reported to have told a friend one time that she would rather see her children out begging in the streets than to see her husband go into politics. Rajiv simply believed that his mother needed him and that he could not leave her. The presence of her family, especially her grandchildren, helped Indira Gandhi eventually to come out of her deep depression over losing the 1977 elections.

6

Reluctant Politician

The new government repealed the emergency decrees and the repressive laws that had been passed during the state of emergency. In foreign relations, the Desai government was warmer to the West and cooler to Moscow and Peking. The government also arrested and tried to convict Mrs. Gandhi on charges of official corruption. She was freed pending a trial.

After her release, the government suspended Sanjay Gandhi's pilot's license, fearing that he might try to fly himself and his mother out of the country. The government also started an investigation into Sanjay's Maruti business. Among the people called to testify was Sanjay's father-in-law, Colonel Anand. The investigation upset the older man, and when he was found dead, a revolver in his hand, there was some question over whether he had committed suicide or had been murdered. Colonel Anand had left a strange note that read: "Pressure Sanjay unbearable." People wondered what that meant: That Sanjay had put pressure on his father-in-law? That the pressure on Sanjay was too much for his father-in-law to bear? Colonel Anand's death under mysterious circumstances did not help Sanjay's reputation.

Once released from prison, Mrs. Gandhi wasted no time seeking a return to power. In early 1978 she and her supporters broke away from the regular Congress party and formed what was known as the Indian National Congress-I (the "I" for Indira) party. That summer, the special commission investigating her conduct while in office charged her with having illegally detained opposition leaders during the emergency. The commission also charged Sanjay Gandhi with having engaged in illegal destruction of private property. And in December, the commission charged Indira Gandhi with harassing four government officials who had been investigating Maruti, Ltd., Sanjay's automobile company.

In Parliament, Prime Minister Desai moved that Mrs. Gandhi be expelled from Parliament and jailed for the remainder of the session. As the vote neared, it became apparent that Mrs. Gandhi still had considerable popular support; there were riots in several cities in protest. The vote, taken in early 1979, was 279 to 138 in favor of the motion. Mrs. Gandhi refused to go home to await arrest. She insisted on being arrested right there in Parliament, and after about three hours she was.

There were more riots and even an airplane hijacking in protest over her arrest. The opposition, fearing more violence, released her when the parliamentary sessions ended.

Mrs. Gandhi worked to reunite the Congress party and to merge her Congress-I party with the older Congress party. Meanwhile, she watched as Prime Minister Desai's government had no better luck solving India's problems than she had and internal problems destroyed the ruling coalition. In July 1979, Prime Minister Desai resigned. Charan Singh, a member of the Cabinet, took over as caretaker prime minister, and new elections were called for January 1980.

By this time, both Indira Gandhi and Sanjay were free to make sure she was returned to power in those elections. In the end, the investigation into Maruti, Ltd., had turned up no real evidence against Sanjay. Nor had the investigation into Indira Gandhi and her government succeeded in making a strong case against her. Critics charged that such evidence existed but that both Gandhis remained so popular in India the opposition feared full-scale riots if either was ever brought to trial.

While managing his mother's campaign, Sanjay also undertook his first political contest, running for the parliamentary seat from Amethi in the state of Uttar Pradesh. In the elections, Indira and her Congress-I party won two-thirds of the seats in Parliament. Sanjay won election to Parliament from Amethi. The way seemed open for Indira Gandhi to rule India again and to further her plans for a family political dynasty. Five months later, in mid-June, Sanjay was made one of the general secretaries of the Congress-I party.

Meanwhile, he was enjoying power and not paying much attention to his responsibilities. Even Maneka had long complained that he did not have enough time for her. In 1979 they had a son, who was named Feroze after his father. But even after Feroze was born, Sanjay, who was then in his early thirties, continued to act at times more like a teenager than as a politician and family man. When he was not acting in an official capacity, he seemed not to care about how his public behavior would be perceived. For a long time, he had hung around with a group of young men whom even the kindest observers called wild. And his own behavior was often irresponsible.

As "unofficial prime minister," as some people called him, he had no business flying small airplanes because it was too risky. But that didn't stop him from doing so. Earlier, a British-Asian industrialist named Swaraj Paul had sent Sanjay a gift of a red Pitts S-2A, an American-made two-seater airplane. By the time it arrived in India, the Indira Gandhi government had been defeated, and the new government charged that the gift was inappropriate. Before a decision had been reached about what to do with the plane, Mrs. Gandhi was returned to office and Sanjay had his plane back. Sanjay decided to take the plane out for a test flight on the morning of June 23, 1980. He took as his passenger Captain Shubhash Saxena, an experienced pilot. On their arrival at the Delhi Flying Club, the club's chief instructor told Sanjay he didn't think it was a good idea to take the Pitts S-2A up, for it had not been test-flown by the club's mechanics. But Sanjay insisted, "I must take up this red bird today."

Sanjay flew the plane over the prime minister's residence and over Willingdon Crescent, where the family had stayed while his mother was out of office. Then he decided to impress his passenger with a few somersaults. The small plane crashed into some trees near Willingdon Crescent. Sanjay and Saxena died instantly.

It was a terrible blow for Indira Gandhi. Sanjay had been her favorite and her heir apparent. She wrote to a friend in the United States, "It is to Sanjay's credit that he retained his dignity and calmness of spirit and to the end was a help and a joy to have around the house."

It was also a terrible blow for Rajiv. He and Sanjay may not have agreed on many things, but they were still brothers. In the small Nehru-Gandhi family, they both had felt the responsibility of being the only remaining men. At the time of Sanjay's death, Rajiv and Sonia and their children were in Italy. They made hasty plans to return, for as the older and the only remaining son, it was Rajiv's duty to preside over the funeral.

In the meantime, Sanjay's body was embalmed. Oddly, even as his body was being preserved, his reputation was being reformed. His enemies now had nothing but nice things to say about him. A member of an opposition party that Sanjay had denounced as corrupt put it this way, "All political controversies are still in the face of death." The death of Sanjay Gandhi suddenly became a national tragedy, and the crowds that turned out for his funeral were unprecedented in size.

By Hindu tradition, the dead are cremated. Indira Gandhi wanted her son's body cremated on the same site as Jawaharlal Nehru's had been, but the political opposition drew the line here. Instead, the funeral pyre was laid well behind the Nehru site. Afterward, Sanjay's ashes were scattered in the Ganges River near Allahabad.

Rajiv presided over it all. It was clear by the way the thousands who attended the funeral bowed to him as he passed by that already people were looking to him to take the place of Sanjay in the Nehru-Gandhi family political dynasty. It was also clear that his mother expected him to take the place of her dead younger son.

Sanjay's widow, Maneka, had her own political ambitions, and she felt that she should succeed her late husband as the member of Parliament from Amethi in Uttar Pradesh. However, since she fell short by fourteen months of the age requirement of thirty, Maneka hoped that the Congress-I party would put someone in the office as caretaker until she was old enough to take over the office. But Indira Gandhi wanted Rajiv to take Sanjay's place. So did her Congress-I party. Three hundred members of Parliament, all of them members of the

After Sanjay's death, his widow Maneka had her own political ambitions.

Congress-I party, sent a petition urging him to take Sanjay's place. Rajiv refused. He was not interested in politics or in family political dynasties. He had not even participated in his mother's or brother's 1980 election campaigns. His wife, Sonia, was against his entering politics. Therefore, he saw no reason to take over as the member of Parliament from Amethi.

No one seemed to understand his reasons. After a while, there were rumors that what he really wanted to do was be a power behind the scenes. Implied in those rumors was that he was sneaky and unwilling to take his knocks in public the way Sanjay had. Rajiv realized that these rumors would eventually do harm to his mother, and that, at this point, Indira Gandhi was insistent that he run for Parliament. At length, he gave in for the sake of his mother. He explained in an interview in *India Today,* "She had a lot of support from Sanjay and now it's not there. . . . I don't know much about politics, so there's no question of my stepping into his shoes." By this he meant that he was willing to help his mother but he didn't intend to be as politically active as Sanjay had been.

In May 1981 Rajiv resigned from Indian Airlines and began to campaign for his brother's seat in Parliament. His wife, Sonia, realized that she must give in. She quietly gave up her Italian citizenship and became a citizen of India at last. In June 1981, a year after his brother's tragic death, Rajiv stood for a special election in Uttar Pradesh and won his brother's seat in Parliament in a landslide victory. He also took Sanjay's place on the executive committee of the Congress-I party's youth wing.

Meanwhile, Maneka, was furious that Rajiv had been chosen instead of her. She began meeting with leaders of opposition groups and considered trying to break Sanjay's followers away from the Congress-I party. She also began to talk about her son, Feroze Varuna, as a future prime minister of India. Such an event was far into the future, of course, as Feroze Varuna was only two years old. But naturally this kind of talk led to tensions in the Gandhi household.

Rajiv liked the idea that he had won such a big victory, but it also left him with a feeling of responsibility to the people he was to represent. He told Trevor Fishlock of *The Times* of London, "Yes, I do feel excited about going into politics. But daunted, too. Look at the people in this constituency. They have so little and there is so much to be done. How do you begin to make improvements? It will be satisfying to make progress, but I have no illusions about the difficulties."

Rajiv began helping his mother. He screened her appointments, advised her on the affairs of her party, and received petitions on her behalf. He tried to get her to stop consulting astrologers about political decisions, telling her, "We aren't living in the Flintstone age." He could not, however, get her to listen to him on that subject. But as the months passed, Mrs. Gandhi often referred party aides to her son, and it was clear that she was depending on him for help.

Maneka Gandhi became more and more resentful. She complained that her mother-in-law was ignoring her. Asked why she did not take her son and leave the household, she hinted that she planned to do just that when the time was right. Finally, in March 1982, she did walk out, amid great publicity. A short time later she announced the formation of the "Sanjay Forum," an organization that would work for "socialism, secularism, and democracy." A year later she formed a political party called the National Sanjay Organization and announced that she would fight Rajiv Gandhi for the parliamentary seat from Amethi.

Meanwhile, in February 1983, Mrs. Gandhi formally

named Rajiv as one of her party's general secretaries. Now that he had an official post in the Congress-I party, Rajiv became more of a public figure, traveling widely both abroad and in India with his mother on official trips. In December of that year he was presented to the Congress party's delegates in the city of Calcutta as the future leader of the country. Posters were put up with a picture of Indira and Rajiv together. Another poster featured Rajiv alone, with the slogan, "Today's Leader, Tomorrow's Hope."

Such publicity was welcome for any politician. But in his calm and quiet way, Rajiv was beginning to establish his own

Indira Gandhi worked hard to push Rajiv, her only remaining son, to the forefront of her ruling party.

reputation in Indian politics, not just as the son of Indira Gandhi but as an able leader in his own right. He gained the respect of the Congress-I party members by being accessible and willing to listen to their advice as well as their problems. He was not universally liked, however, because he clearly wanted to reorganize the party, bringing in young politicians and professional managers and improving its image. He wanted to put the charges of bribery and corruption behind and to raise the standards of the party. He himself developed a reputation as an upholder of higher standards of morality and performance than the average Congress party politician. In fact, he'd been given the nickname, "Mr. Clean."

Older Indians thought they recognized in Rajiv some of the idealism of his grandfather, Jawaharlal Nehru. But they wondered if his mother's realism and toughness might not be better suited to the rough-and-tumble nature of Indian politics.

In June 1984, Prime Minister Indira Gandhi showed her toughness when she ordered Indian troops to invade the Golden Temple of Amritsar in the Punjab. The temple, the holiest shrine of the Sikhs, had been taken over by Sikh extremists protesting Hindu rule in the state. They were led by the most militant Sikh leader, Jarnail Singh Bhindranwale. Indira Gandhi decided that the only way to get them out was by force. During the siege at the seventy-two-acre complex, there were heavy losses on both sides. But the government eventually routed the Sikh terrorists from the temple. The majority of Indians approved of Mrs. Gandhi's swift action to put down the terrorism, but some among the Sikh minority vowed revenge.

7

Assassination

On the morning of October 31, 1984, Prime Minister Indira Gandhi awakened as usual around six o'clock and drank a pot of hot tea while she read quickly through a variety of local Hindi and English-language newspapers. She did her morning exercises, bathed and dressed, and then joined Sonia and Rahul and Priyanka for breakfast. Rajiv was in West Bengal on a campaign trip that morning.

Mrs. Gandhi asked her grandchildren how they were feeling. The evening before, the car in which they had been riding had been rammed by a van that had run a red light. The children were not hurt, and the prime minister's security guards assured her that there was nothing suspicious about the incident. Still, the accident had troubled Mrs. Gandhi, and she had canceled all her appointments, except one, for the next day. Later that night she had sat at her desk and written these words: "I have never felt less like dying and that calm and peace of mind is what prompts me to write what is in the nature of a will. If I die a violent death as some fear and a few are plotting, I know the violence will be in the thought and action of the assassin, not in my dying—for no hate is dark enough to overshadow the extent of my love for my people and my country; no force is strong enough to divert me from my purpose and my endeavor to take this country forward."

The children were fine that morning and talked happily about what they were going to do that day. Mrs. Gandhi's secretary came to the dining room and spoke with her about the one appointment she had not canceled. She kissed and hugged her grandchildren and went with her secretary to her study. Her only appointment was with an actor named Peter Ustinov. He was filming a series called "Ustinov's People" for American television, and he wanted to interview her on the lawns behind the official residence.

At 9:15 A.M., Mrs. Gandhi stepped out of her home. A New Delhi policeman held an umbrella over her head to protect her from the sun. She was not wearing her bullet-proof vest under her orange cotton sari. Her secretary walked behind them. As Mrs. Gandhi neared a hedge, she saw Beant Singh, a twenty-eight-year-old Sikh policeman who had been part of her security guard for six years. She smiled at him. He moved closer to her, then quickly drew a pistol and fired three shots at point-blank range. Before her body slumped to the ground, another Sikh guard, twenty-one-year-old Satwant Singh, a member of the New Delhi police force, appeared and let loose with an automatic carbine rifle. Then both guards dropped their weapons and raised their hands in surrender. "We have done what we set out to do," said Beant Singh in Hindi. "Now you can do whatever you want to do."

But everyone else was too horrified to act. They had dived for cover. Sonia Gandhi now ran from the house. She and the prime minister's secretary lifted Mrs. Gandhi into a nearby car and raced to the All-India Institute of Medical Sciences. There, doctors worked frantically to save her life, but there were thirty-two bullets in her body. Five hours after the shooting, Prime Minister Indira Gandhi was officially declared dead.

In the meantime, her two assassins had remained standing, hands raised in the air, until someone decided to arrest them. They were taken to a guardhouse. Beant Singh was shot and killed there when he tried to escape. Satwant Singh was hanged in 1989, along with Kehar Singh, a coconspirator.

At the time Mrs. Gandhi was being taken to the hospital, Rajiv Gandhi was addressing a huge rally in Contai in the state of West Bengal, more than a thousand miles away. He was on his way to another rally when his motorcade was stopped by a police jeep, and he was told of the assassination attempt. A number of Congress party members around him began to cry, but Rajiv did not. He comforted them as he turned the dials of his portable radio for news. The British Broadcasting Corporation station was reporting that Indira Gandhi was already dead. But the All-India Radio network was playing Hindu music. "It's all very confusing," said Rajiv. Eventually, a helicopter arrived to pick him up and take him to Calcutta, where an Air Force jet was waiting to take him to New Delhi. He reached the institute an hour and a half after his mother had been officially declared dead.

By the time he arrived, crowds had gathered outside the institute, and mobs of Hindus were attacking every Sikh in sight. The men were easy to spot in their traditional long hair, beards, and turbans, and they were being pulled off buses and motorcycles and beaten up. As news of the assassination spread across the huge land, Hindus in other cities also formed mobs and attacked Sikhs, and there were reports of mob violence and killings of Sikhs, as well as attacks on Sikh shrines in Calcutta, Madras, Kanpur, and Agartala, capital of Tripura State.

67

In London, Dr. Jagjit Singh Chohan, who described himself as the president of the Sikh government of Kalistan in exile, issued a statement. In it, he said that Mrs. Gandhi had been killed because she had ordered the storming of the Golden Temple of Amritsar in June. "All those responsible for the massacre of thousands of innocent women and children during the assault on the Golden Temple will be taken care of by the Kalistan commando forces," the statement said. It was a clear warning that the killing of Mrs. Gandhi was only the beginning of a campaign of terror against the Indian government by Sikh revolutionaries.

The Indian government acted swiftly to quell the violence. Curfews were ordered, and police and national security forces were put on the alert. The government also acted quickly to fill the office of prime minister. That same day the cabinet held an emergency meeting and unanimously elected Rajiv to be the new prime minister. That night, President Zail Singh, a Sikh, administered the oath of office to Rajiv, who took that oath in English.

Many were surprised that Rajiv was named prime minister so quickly. After the death of Jawaharlal Nehru, and after his successor, Shri Lal Bahadur Shastri, died, the home minister was in each case named interim prime minister. Rajiv Gandhi was a member of Parliament, but he held no cabinet post. Still, the executive committee of the ruling Congress party decided that it was best not to leave any question about who was leading India. Indira Gandhi had wanted her son to succeed her. Her party made sure that he did by making him the new head of the Congress party and therefore prime minister. It would not be official until a formal election was held after Mrs. Gandhi's funeral, but unless something happened to Rajiv in the meantime, he would win that formal election.

For Rajiv Gandhi, there was no time to mourn his

mother. He had to step in and be the new leader of India. That very evening, he gave his first speech as prime minister:

"Indira Gandhi, India's prime minister, has been assassinated. She was mother not only to me but to the whole nation. She served the Indian people to the last drop of her blood. . . .

"This is a moment of profound grief. The foremost need now is to maintain our balance. We can and must face this tragic ordeal with fortitude, courage and wisdom. We should remain calm and exercise the maximum restraint. We should not let our emotions get the better of us, because passion would cloud judgment.

"Nothing would hurt the soul of our beloved Indira Gandhi more than the occurrence of violence in any part of the country. . . .

"Indira Gandhi is no more, but her soul lives. India lives. India is immortal. I know that the nation will recognize its responsibilities and that we shall shoulder the burden heroically and with determination.

"The nation has placed a great responsibility on me by asking me to head the government. I shall be able to fulfill it only with your support and cooperation. I shall value your guidance in upholding the unity, integrity and honor of the country."

There were some who questioned how the integrity and honor of India as a democracy could possibly continue now that Rajiv Gandhi had been named prime minister. After all, it was not democratic to rule by family dynasty. Charan Singh, the former prime minister who had failed to hold an opposition government together in 1979 and 1980 and who had thus let Mrs. Gandhi return after three years out of power, complained that "democracy is being gradually eroded in the country in order to establish a dynastic rule."

But others felt that making Rajiv the new prime minister was a smart move. After all, he had not been in politics long enough to have made many enemies. And his campaign promises back in 1980 to rid Indian politics of corruption were still associated with him, as well as the nickname "Mr. Clean." It was hoped that he would somehow give a sense of stability to the country and that the people would rally around him because he was the son of their slain leader and the grandson of the man who was remembered as the father of India, Jawaharlal Nehru.

There was no question that India needed stable leadership in those first days after the assassination of Indira Gandhi. There was unrest and violence everywhere, and Indian army troops were ordered into nine cities where rioting was the worst. In New Delhi, the leaders of the opposition parties released a joint statement with Prime Minister Rajiv Gandhi appealing for an end to the violence. In Pakistan, President Mohammad Zia ul-Haq made a public offer to Gandhi to help create an atmosphere of trust between their two countries. Rajiv appreciated all these offers of support, but first he had to oversee the funeral of his mother.

Indira Gandhi's body lay in state in a house that had once been her father's, not far from the official residence. Thousands of mourners filed by, some bringing bunches of flowers. Meanwhile, at the Indian Parliament, Rajiv Gandhi was officially confirmed as prime minister. His first official act as prime minister coincided with his official role as the only son of Indira Gandhi. He presided at a huge state funeral attended by representatives from fifty countries, including United States Secretary of State George Shultz and Pakistan President Mohammad Zia ul-Haq.

The funeral was carried live on Indian television. Some people suggested that this was the reason for the poor attendance at the funeral by ordinary Indians. For the funerals of Mohandas Gandhi in 1948, Jawaharlal Nehru in 1964, and Lal Bahadur Shastri in 1966, the crowds along the funeral route had been several persons deep. Even Sanjay Gandhi's funeral had been better attended than that of his mother. Others suggested that people had stayed away because of possible violence. They pointed out that few Sikhs dared attend the funeral. Even Sikh priests who had been invited had not accepted.

Maneka Gandhi, and her five-year-old son, Feroze Varuna, stood next to Rajiv and his family. She planned to

Rajiv stands at the funeral pyre of his mother, flanked by his wife, Sonia, and his children, Rahul and Priyana.

run against her brother-in-law in the parliamentary elections the next year. But for the time being they were family, not political opponents.

Mother Teresa was there. She came from Calcutta to offer a prayer that Mrs. Gandhi would live in peace forever. An Anglican Church bishop recited the Twenty-third Psalm. A Moslem malvi spoke. Hindu pandits chanted mantras. There was a real attempt to include all of India's faiths at the funeral.

Afterward, the priests and family and invited guests accompanied the body to the cremation grounds. Rajiv lit the funeral pyre.

According to traditional Hindu practice, the ashes are deposited in one of India's holy rivers. The family of the deceased then mourns for ten days, and after that time the soul of the dead person is believed to have entered a new body. If the dead person lived a good life, then the new life on earth will be even better. If not, the soul is punished by being caused to live a harder life the next time around. But for Indira Gandhi, things were handled a bit differently.

Her ashes were put into urns that were set aboard special trains to be taken to all Indian states before most were scattered on the Himalayas. One small urn was buried under a tree on the family estate at Allahabad.

Rajiv Gandhi was not able to spend ten days at home in mourning. He had a riot-torn country to run. He met immediately with a delegation of prominent Sikhs to try to defuse the tensions in his country. He assured these Sikhs that he did not believe the men who had assassinated his mother represented all Sikhs and that they were "two misguided individuals." He called for peace.

Meanwhile, however, one of the six Sikhs arrested in the plot had told police that if Rajiv had been with his mother

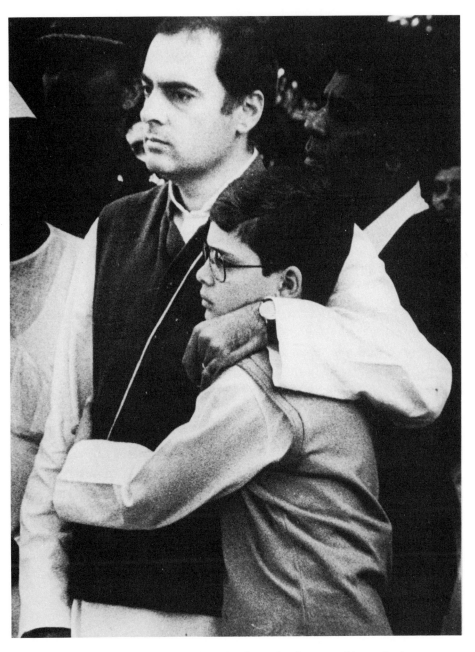

Rajiv comforts his son, Rahul, as he faces the future as his mother's successor.

that morning of October 31, he would have been assassinated also, and so the security around Rajiv was extraordinary. When Rajiv went to the Nehru family estate in Allahabad in northern India, however, to bury the urn filled with his mother's ashes, there were no incidents.

Rajiv was in constant contact with Indian army commanders and police officials in the areas of greatest turmoil. He was relieved to learn from many of them that the riots in their areas were not as a result of the general population going crazy. Rather, it was young hoodlums who seemed to be the worst offenders. There were reports, too, that many Hindus were helping the Sikhs by hiding them and trying to protect them. Still, hundreds had been killed, thousands more injured.

Soon, the violence had pretty much ended. The curfews were relaxed in the areas where they had been imposed. In New Delhi the beggars and merchants were back on the streets. By the time the ashes of the slain prime minister were scattered on the mountains and buried at Allahabad, her country was almost as peaceful as it had ever been known to be.

As Rajiv buried the urn filled with his mother's ashes, he symbolized two very different things. In one way, he represented the continuity of the family political dynasty and the direct blood line from his grandfather, through his mother, to himself. But in another way, he represented a break with the past. Rajiv Gandhi was one of "midnight's children," the first leader of India to have come of age in an independent India, a prime minister who had no direct experience in the struggle for independence from Britain.

8

Prime Minister Rajiv Gandhi

On November 12, 1984, after the official period of mourning, Rajiv was unanimously elected president of the Congress-I party. In his first national policy speech, he called for national unity, world peace, continuation of Indian socialism and planning, promotion of science and technology, and adoption of a "new work ethic." By the last item he hoped to encourage people to work harder so that they, and India, would prosper.

The following day, the government announced that national elections would be held at the end of December. This was a full month earlier than the constitution required, but Rajiv wanted to be elected prime minister by the people as soon as possible. His campaign theme was "national unity," and he toured the country by helicopter, trying to see and be seen by as many people as possible.

Then, in the midst of the campaign, a tragedy occurred at Bhopal. On December 3 poisonous gas leaks from an American-owned Union Carbide insecticide plant caused the deaths of as many as 2,500 people in the city of Bhopal. Rajiv flew there immediately and ordered emergency measures to aid the victims and to stop the spread of the poisonous gas. He instructed government attorneys to demand compensation from Union Carbide for the victims and their families. He also promised that his government would review its policies regarding the location of factories that produced hazardous chemicals. The Bhopal disaster was one of the worst tragedies ever caused by humans but no one blamed the Indian government, and especially not Rajiv.

The elections at the end of December were for him what one news source described as "the most complete, comprehensive triumph" in India's history. Although Congress-I candidates received only 49 percent of the total popular vote, they got far more votes than any of the opposition candidates. Congress-I candidates won 401 of the 508 seats that were contested in that election in the lower house of Parliament, the Lok Sabha (House of the People). Elections for seats representing Punjab and Bhopal had been postponed because of the problems in those areas.

Rajiv ran again for his seat from Amethi, opposed by his sister-in-law, Maneka. He won by over 300,000 votes. With this victory, he retained leadership of the Congress-I party, and because the Congress-I party had won a majority in Parliament, he also retained the office of prime minister.

Outside observers explained his victory by saying that it was due partly to sympathy over his mother's death, partly to the fact that the opposition parties were disorganized, and also to the fact that he had no real political enemies. In some ways, his inexperience in politics was an advantage. He did not come to office with baggage from his mother's long reign. He was not associated with her excesses. Until practically forced to enter the political arena, he had made no public political statements and few if any private ones. People who knew him well in the late 1970s could not remember his ever

Rajiv speaks at a campaign rally before the December 1984 election that officially made him Prime Minister.

saying one word about politics. They could not even say for sure whether he had ever talked politics with Sanjay.

Rajiv was formally inaugurated as prime minister on December 31, 1984. Also inaugurated on that day were thirty-nine ministers whose duties were to oversee various aspects of life in India. Like his grandfather and his mother before him, Rajiv chose to conduct foreign affairs himself. He let it be known, however, that he would keep a close watch on all government activities and would dismiss any minister who was not doing his job. He also appointed a special cabinet group to deal with the problem of the Punjab. In his view, his biggest challenge was national unity.

In early 1985 he dismissed some of the men who had been chief aides to his mother. He replaced them with young Western-educated men whose background was business and technology. Some people charged that Rajiv was trying to run India like a corporation. Others said that wasn't such a bad idea.

Leaving his ministers in charge of affairs on the home front, at least for the time being, Rajiv turned his attention to international affairs. He did a lot of traveling in May. He visited the Soviet Union and signed two trade agreements. In doing so, he assured the Russians that the special relationship between the two countries that his grandfather had established and that his mother had strengthened would remain intact.

After that he traveled to the United States. He spoke to a joint session of Congress and met privately with President Ronald Reagan. He criticized American military aid to Pakistan, in public and also in private. He quietly began negotiations to buy United States military equipment. He wanted to deal with whomever could help India and did not want to be hampered by traditional politics.

Rajiv and Sonia paid an official visit to the Soviet Union in July 1987 and met with General Secretary Mikhail Gorbachev and his wife, Raisa.

That same summer, Rajiv and Sonia visited the United States. Secretary of State George Shultz and his wife greeted them at Andrews Air Force Base.

Back in India, he attended to the negotiations over the Punjab. In late July 1985 the Indian government signed a major agreement with Sikh leaders there that gave Sikhs, who were in the majority in the region, more say in the politics and the economy of the Punjab. Not all Sikhs approved of the agreement. In August, a moderate Sikh leader was assassinated by Sikh extremists. There were also threats against Rajiv.

Unlike his mother, who had refused extra protection, Rajiv took these threats seriously. He moved his family out of Teen Murti and into the historic Red Fort in the old city of Delhi. It was surrounded by security forces. His children were tutored at home instead of attending local schools. When he addressed the nation on Independence Day, he stood at a podium encased in bulletproof glass. In that speech, he announced that a settlement similar to that for the Punjab had been reached with the oil-rich and tea-growing state of Assam, where illegal immigrants from neighboring Bangladesh had been causing unrest for years and where the native Assamese had worried that they would become a minority in their own state. "Ten months ago the world was watching whether India will disintegrate into pieces," he told the nation. "Today that question does not arise. The world now finds a strong India."

There were other reasons why Rajiv Gandhi could so confidently proclaim his nation a united one. He had consulted with opposition party leaders and kept them informed of all his decisions. When Indira Gandhi had been prime minister, the opposition had usually been left out of major decisions and in turn had been loudly critical. There was hardly any criticism in Parliament of Rajiv Gandhi.

In September 1985 elections were held at last in the Punjab. The Congress-I party lost, but Rajiv was pleased nevertheless. The Akali Dal party, which won the elections, was moderate. He could work with its leaders. He described the results of the election as a victory for democracy and nonviolence.

Rajiv was pleased with what his special cabinet group had accomplished in the Punjab and Assam. He was not so pleased with how things were going in other areas of the home front. He reorganized and expanded his council of ministers, increasing the number from thirty-nine to fifty-one and dismissing those who opposed him. He later explained, "I tried at the beginning for about a year to carry all the groups with us. But I found you couldn't get things done if you tried to carry all the groups with you. . . . Also, I found that the opposition was seldom coming out with concrete guidance on policy. . . . If I call together opposition leaders . . . and ask for ideas . . . they have no ideas at all. It's all negative." He also gave over the day-to-day running of foreign affairs to ministers. He chose now to concentrate on defense.

He had information that Pakistan was either in the process of making, or had already made, a nuclear bomb. His sources had reported that Pakistan had the enriched uranium necessary for production. India, he said, had possessed the technology to build the bomb since the 1970s. Back then, the decision had been made not to build it. But India could change its mind.

Rajiv also had information that Pakistan was buying gas masks in Europe and was setting up a factory to produce its own gas masks.

In the face of both the nuclear and chemical threats from Pakistan, Rajiv believed that he had to concentrate on his nation's ability to protect itself. In New York in October 1985, on the occasion of the fortieth anniversary of the United Nations, he met with Pakistan's President Mohammad Zia ul-Haq, and while nothing major came of this meeting, the fact that the two leaders were talking was a step in the right direction.

Later in India, Rajiv carried a torch in ceremonies marking the first anniversary of the assassination of his mother. Looking back on his first year in office, many observers marveled at how quickly the memory of Indira Gandhi had receded. Her quiet, nonpolitical son had put his own strong mark on India now. A year earlier, very few had expected that he could.

9

New Troubles

A new leader's first year in office is usually the easiest. In fact, it is often called a "honeymoon." People are willing to give the new leader a chance and will support his or her efforts. Rajiv Gandhi's first year as prime minister was such a honeymoon period. When it was over, the problems he thought he'd at least started to solve began to crop up again.

After a short period of calm, the Punjab was in turmoil once more. Some 450 people died there in 1986 alone as a result of the unrest. Rajiv Gandhi was angry that his attempts at working out a peaceful solution had failed. Now he tried some of his mother's tactics. He sent more police to the Punjab and ordered a crackdown on terrorism. There were police sweeps of towns and villages. More than fifty Sikh lawmakers were arrested in addition to many other militants. In retaliation, Sikh militants killed police. Ordinary people, caught in the middle, fled their homes and became refugees.

The problem in the Punjab seemed to spill over into other parts of the country as agitators for different causes became increasingly militant. In the western state of Gujarat, violence among Hindus, Moslems, and lower caste groups resulted in the deaths of 250 people in the first months of 1986. In Goa, a tiny former Portuguese colony on India's western coast, there were riots by rebels demanding statehood for Goa. At the same time, Gurkhas in northeastern India were agitating for statehood as well. There were daily reports of killings and demonstrations and battles among workers on the tea plantations in the area.

In the southern state of Tamil Nadu, bombs were set off by protesters against Hindi as the national language. Twenty years earlier, there had been talk of secession by Tamil Nadu, and the latest round of violence signaled new unrest.

Indian government representatives charged that much of this unrest was the work of a small, highly organized group of terrorists who were bent on destroying India's fragile unity. But whether or not that was the cause, the unrest continued.

It was not Rajiv Gandhi's fault, nor had it been the fault of his mother and grandfather before him. India was a country created not by Indians but by the British. They had conquered a large geographical area, and their mapmakers had drawn up the boundaries of a colony called India without regard for the communities within those boundaries. While Britain had ruled, it had managed to impose unity. Once Britain left, the divisions had resurfaced. The Indian subcontinent had split in two (Pakistan) and then in three (Bangladesh).

Some of the problems caused by factionalism also spilled over into India's foreign relations. When Rajiv Gandhi accused Pakistan of training and arming Sikh terrorists in an attempt to undermine his government, the problem in the Punjab became an international one.

In January 1987, 340,000 Indian and Pakistani troops faced off along a 250-mile stretch of their shared border. A hasty visit to New Delhi by Pakistan's president, Mohammad

Zia ul-Haq, squelched the fears of war for the time being, but the troops remained at the border. Critics of Gandhi in both India and Pakistan accused him of deliberately increasing tensions between the two countries in order to divert attention from his problems at home. At the same time, the difficulties between India and Pakistan threatened to endanger India's relations with the United States, a supporter of General Zia of Pakistan.

Rajiv had made the economy of India one of his top priorities, stressing modernization and outside investment. He believed that industry would do better if operated by private sources rather than by the government. His efforts were showing some positive results. Many industries had started to boom, exports had increased, and there were more consumer products available for those who could afford them. For the first time since independence in 1947, India was on its way to having *more,* not less than it needed, of things like cement, synthetic textiles, and electronics.

But so far, only India's small middle class had benefited from these changes. The masses of poor people saw no difference in their hard lives. Gandhi hoped the effects of the industrial boom would eventually "trickle down" to the poor, but hundreds of millions of them were not even in a position to benefit from the "money economy." They could barely make ends meet by growing their own food and trading it for things they needed, like clothing. They had nothing left over to trade for money, and so they had no money to buy the increasingly available consumer products.

Prime Minister Gandhi realized that his economic reforms were not reaching the poor people. He hoped that the increased taxes paid to the government by the booming industries would help fund programs for the needy. But critics charged that he should put the needs of the poor first. They said he was sacrificing the poor in favor of business interests. Gandhi's former finance minister, Pranab Mukherjee, who had been fired by Gandhi after he disagreed with the prime minister's policies, stated, "There are 31,000 villages without [drinkable] water, and this government is concerned about having more television centers and more computers for our research institutions. Is that where priorities should be?"

To make matters worse for Rajiv Gandhi, even some of his new technology developments did not work. In the spring of 1986 India's first intercontinental rocket crashed less than three minutes into its maiden flight. Some critics saw the failure of the rocket as symbolic of the failure of Rajiv's government.

His finance minister was not the only member of the government who was angry with the prime minister. Zail Singh, India's president, accused Gandhi of not living up to his constitutional duty of keeping him informed.

The prime minister's power depended greatly on the continued power of his Congress-I party, and the party wasn't doing very well. While it continued to hold the seats in Parliament that it had won in the landslide victory of December 1984, it had lost a number of state and local elections by the fall of 1986. By then, it could claim local control in only twelve of twenty-three states.

Rajiv Gandhi himself was still popular. Educated people understood that the problems he faced were the same ones that had plagued India since independence. There was too much poverty, too many people, and too little education. There were too many divisions based on religion and caste. And there was the old political bureaucracy—inefficient and full of corruption and special interests. In India, nothing was simple if it involved the government. Even the families of the victims of Bhopal had not yet gotten the money promised to them. The American company, Union Carbide, had paid millions to the government, but that money had not percolated through all the layers of government to the people it was meant to help.

Poor, uneducated people didn't really blame Rajiv Gandhi either. After all, he was a politician. In their view, all politicians were ineffective.

In this belief both poor, uneducated people and middle class, educated people agreed. In Indian government, the amazing thing is that anything ever gets done.

The problem, according to Nani A. Palkhivala, a senior

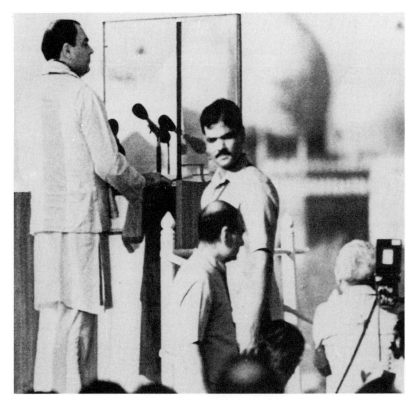

Rajiv stood behind bulletproof glass and was surrounded by bodyguards as he spoke on the occasion of the 40th anniversary of Indian independence.

advocate in the Supreme Court of India, is that India as a nation has no sense of time. He wrote in an op-editorial in the *Times* of London in August 1987, "In the national language, Hindi, the same word—*kal*—is used for both yesterday and tomorrow. Ancient India had evolved the concepts of eternity and infinity and our bureaucracy conforms with the hypothesis that we live in eternity. . . . Files and minutes [records of meetings] still go perpetually from ministry to ministry . . . Millions of man-hours are wasted every day in coping with inane bureaucratic regulations and a torrential spate of amendments."

But it takes more than lack of blame to make a strong leader. Observers inside and outside India were beginning to think that Rajiv Gandhi just wasn't up to his job. His quiet, shy way had been refreshing after the toughness of his mother. But now people suspected that he might be weak and indecisive.

Government bureaucrats were furious at his constant public attacks against the system. They were angry, too, that he seemed to rely for advice on old school chums with little political experience. In the beginning, some observers had hoped that new ideas from these younger, Western-educated men would help solve some of India's problems. When these observers saw no progress, they decided that Gandhi and his advisers were a bunch of amateurs. Around Delhi, political insiders had taken to calling him "the Boy."

The Gandhi government seemed to reach a low point in June 1987 when the Congress-I party candidate lost a crucial election in the state of Haryana. Many observers had looked to that election as the key to the prime minister's future. Rajiv Gandhi, in fact, considered the election so important that he had personally made two trips to Haryana to campaign for Congress-I party candidates. But an alliance of two opposition parties, the People's party and the National People's party, won forty-two of the fifty-one seats contested. The head of the People's party announced, "This is the final notice from the people of India to Mr. Gandhi to quit."

But Rajiv Gandhi had no intention of quitting. In fact, he was about to take a bold foreign policy step.

Off the southeastern coast of India is the island nation of Sri Lanka, once known as Ceylon. The Buddhist Sinhalese make up the majority of the population, but there is a large minority of Tamils, who are Hindus. For years, the Tamils have been demanding more rights. India has supported them, for in India there are about fifty million Tamils, predominantly in the southeastern state of Tamil Nadu. In 1983 tensions between the Sinhalese and Tamils had erupted into full-scale civil war, and by 1987 some six thousand people had died. The Tamil guerrillas had been using Tamil Nadu as a base and had been receiving arms and supplies from sympathizers there. The war threatened the stability of the entire area.

Rajiv Gandhi, like his mother and grandfather before him, very much wanted India to be known as a regional superpower. He decided that it was up to India to bring about peace in Sri Lanka. In July he ordered his representatives to engage in secret talks with the Sri Lankan government. Three weeks later, he and the president of Sri Lanka, Junius R. Jayawardene, signed an agreement that promised to end the civil war.

Under the agreement, Jayawardene conceded local rule in two provinces heavily populated by Tamils. Gandhi promised to make sure that the Tamil rebels would lay down their arms and sent Indian peace-keeping forces into the Tamil strongholds. It was an important, and historic, agreement. Around the world, Gandhi and Jayawardene were applauded for their statesmanship and courage.

But it remained to be seen whether the agreement could

89

be kept. The Sinhalese were furious with Jayawardene for "caving in" to the Tamils and to India. As Gandhi passed a Sri Lankan honor guard, a sailor broke ranks and swung at the Indian president with the butt end of his rifle. Gandhi caught a blow to his head, but was not seriously injured. In fact, the incident helped him, for it reminded his countrymen that he was in a very dangerous job.

10

From Raj to Rajiv

The signing of the peace agreement between India and Sri Lanka took place at almost the same time as the celebration of the fortieth anniversary of Indian independence, on August 15, 1987. The coincidence was probably no accident. Rajiv Gandhi wanted to mark that anniversary in a special way.

He wished to show the world that India was a major power, strong enough to act as a peacekeeper in its own area of the globe. To that end, he had built up the military so that India would soon be the world's fourth-ranking military power. In fact, some observers remarked that India was fast becoming the India of Rama, the ancient Hindu warrior king. He wanted to show that he was a statesman and that his government could accomplish delicate diplomatic negotiations.

He believed that he, and India, had other things to be proud of on that fortieth anniversary of independence. Chief among them was that the India that was granted independence as a democratic republic in 1947 continued to exist. It was no small victory that after forty years India had survived as a democracy. A land of rajs (maharajahs) and untouch-

91

ables ruled for two hundred years by the British became a land of individual communities and groups lumped with one another inside artificial boundaries and was still somehow holding together. Close to eight hundred million people, more than the combined populations of Africa and South America, more than three times the population of the United States, lived together in freedom as one nation. As Nani A. Palkhivala put it, "Never before, anywhere in the world, has one-sixth of the human race banded itself into a single free nation."

There were still overwhelming contradictions in India and a gap between rich and poor that is hard for outsiders to imagine. That same year, 1987, the son and daughter of two of India's wealthiest and most influential former maharajahs were married in front of twenty thousand guests. No food or drink was served out of sympathy for the victims of drought in northern India.

In the poorer areas of India in 1987, more than one young bride died under mysterious circumstances, either forced to commit suicide or actually killed by her husband's family. Many Indians are so poor and women have so little value in some parts of India that a man will marry a young woman just to collect the dowry, the "bride-price," that her parents must pay to him for marrying her. Once he has the dowry, which is usually livestock, he has no more need of her. In fact, if he can get rid of her, he can marry another young woman and collect another dowry.

India's traditions are on a collision course with modern technology, and there is much resistance to government attempts to modernize the country. When the government decided to import millions of dollars' worth of car telephones and credit card-operated public telephones, explaining that business executives needed such communications systems to

Rajiv speaks at an International Youth Conference Against Apartheid in South Africa, held in New Delhi in early 1987.

operate more efficiently in a growing economy, some critics complained bitterly. They said the money would be better spent on food for the victims of drought.

Critics of the government also didn't think much of government attempts to introduce the five-day work week. They charged that it was for India's small middle class, not for the average worker. Actually, it was mostly aimed at the nearly 3.5 million government employees. The idea was to make them more efficient by giving them two days to rest. Another aim was to cut government expenditures by reducing the use of office cars, air conditioners, room heaters, and overtime pay. Government employees were used to working at least five and a half days, but setting their own hours, so they didn't actually work nine to six every day. Under the new system, they still tended to set their own hours during the official five days and so got less done than they used to.

These problems, of course, are minor compared to the terrible divisiveness and extremist violence that plague India. In his speech to the nation on independence day, Rajiv vowed, "We shall not let our country become hostage to cowardly killers. We rededicate ourselves to preserving our hard-won freedom and waging relentless war on poverty, on prejudice and superstition, on fanaticism and violence, and on all forms of oppression and discrimination." Sadly, he had to wear a bulletproof vest as he gave that speech.

But all the hatred and terror had not torn India apart. Somehow, India seemed to have the strength to endure situations that would cause a revolution in other countries. Its people had not yet developed the habits of tolerance and respect toward each other that a true democracy needs. India still did not have a "national identity." Its people identified themselves by their religion or caste before they called themselves

Indians. Still, after forty years, they were together. It was hoped that they were also maturing together.

Rajiv Gandhi was maturing, too. His critics sometimes forgot that he had not been in politics very long and that he never wanted to be a politician in the first place. Even after three years of being prime minister, he spoke openly of how happy he had been as an airline pilot and hinted that he missed the freedom of private life. "There are still places you can find where nobody can get to you," he told a reporter in the fall of 1987.

How different that life was from his present life. Everywhere he went, he was surrounded by elaborate security. People who wanted to see him had first to go through metal detectors. He and his family lived in a closely guarded compound. His children, teenagers now, still were taught by private tutors and could not come and go freely. Rajiv worried about that sometimes, wondering how it would affect them never to have been able to mix freely with other young people their age. He wondered, too, about how his wife, Sonia, felt. She'd never wanted him to enter politics. She had started wearing saris, the traditional costume for Indian women, and learning Hindi, only because of his position. She, too, was very isolated, guarded round the clock. Both Rajiv and Sonia realized that there were "deep-rooted feelings," as Rajiv put it, about their marriage. Many, many Indians were still troubled by the fact that Rajiv had not taken an Indian wife.

Millions of Indians continued to be concerned by what they perceived as a lack of traditional "Indian-ness" about Rajiv—not only his non-Indian wife, but his upper-class origins, his halting ability in Hindi, the language of most of northern India, and his Western way of looking at things. As V. N. Narayanan, editor in chief of the *Tribune* in Chandigarh, explained in the fall of 1987, "Rajiv is not someone who can address the nation like his mother could. Sanjay was more of the soil. Rajiv has the gentle manners of the West. I wouldn't call him an Oriental person. In that way, he's more like his grandfather than his mother. But Nehru was a cult figure. Rajiv is not."

Rajiv had not come to office willingly. In fact, some people called him "Reluctant Rajiv." He laughed at that nickname and agreed that it described him well. Why did he keep away from politics and from any involvement in Indian government until he was forced into it? "Because there wasn't a need to be involved. The family was involved. It doesn't mean everyone has to get involved. When my brother died there was a need." And when his mother was killed, there was an even greater need.

During his time as prime minister, Rajiv Gandhi had grown in office, learning to juggle the responsibilities of moving his country into the modern age while at the same time carrying on the legacy of his mother and grandfather before him. It was too early to tell how history will judge Rajiv Gandhi. But whether he succeeded or failed, there was no question that he had tried to do his best.

Further Reading

BOOKS

Ali, Tariq. *An Indian Dynasty: The Story of the Nehru-Gandhi Family.* New York: G.P. Putnam's Sons, 1985.

Brown, Joe David. *India.* New York: Time, Inc., 1961.

Gupte, Pranay. *Vengeance: India after the Assassination of Indira Gandhi.* New York: W.W. Norton & Co., 1985.

Mehta, Ved. *A Family Affair: India Under Three Prime Ministers.* New York: Oxford University Press, 1982.

Norman, Dorothy, ed. *Indira Gandhi: Letters to an American Friend, 1950-1984.* San Diego: Harcourt Brace Jovanovich, 1985.

ARTICLES

Charlton, Linda. "Indira Gandhi, Born to Politics, Left Her Own Imprint on India." *The New York Times,* November 1, 1984, pp. 20-22.

Hazarika, Sanjoy. "Son in Charge in New Delhi," *The New York Times,* November 1, 1984, pp. 1+.

Lelyveld, Joseph. "Rajiv, the Son." *The New York Times Magazine,* December 2, 1984, pp. 39-43+.

Margolis, Eric. "Asia Worries About Gandhi's Military Complex." *The Wall Street Journal,* May 2, 1988, p. 25.

Palkhivala, Nani A. "A Passage to Progress." *The London Times,* August 14, 1987.

Rosenthal, A.M. "Father and Daughter: A Remembrance." *The New York Times,* November 1, 1984, pp. 1+.

Smith, William E. "Death in the Garden." *Time,* November 12, 1984, pp. 42-48.

Stevens, William K. "For India, Huge Void." *The New York Times,* November 1, 1984, pp. 1+.

Weisman, Steven R. "India's Tentative Turnaround." *The New York Times,* May 29, 1988, pp. 1+.

"The Rajiv Generation." *The New York Times Magazine,* April 20, 1986, pp. 18-22+.

OTHER

Current Biography Yearbook 1985 New York: The H.W. Wilson Co., pp. 130-134.

Keesing's Contemporary Archives London: Longman. 1972-1985.

Index

101

102

103